I0554854

FIREBIRD

POETRY AND PROSE

FIREBIRD

POETRY AND PROSE

MICHELLE SCHAPER

300 SOUTH MEDIA GROUP
✦✦✦
NEW YORK

FIREBIRD
Copyright © 2022 by Michelle Schaper
All rights reserved.
No part of this book may be reproduced in any form or by any
electronic or mechanical means including information storage
and retrieval systems, without permission in writing from the
author. The only exception is for book reviews or articles written
about the book and/or author.

This book is presented as a collection.

ISBN-13: 978-1-957596-11-2

Author: Michelle Schaper
Book Design & Cover Design: Indie Author Solutions
Published by 300 South Media Group

As always, for my beautiful daughters Chelsea and Tiana

TABLE OF CONTENTS

I wish to start a new pandemic. Call it LOVE and let it spread like wildfire across the world. Symptoms should include kindness and compassion for all.

— Michelle Schaper

THE FIREBIRD MYTH

Stories of the Firebird represent a rare treasure that's difficult to possess symbolising rebirth, beauty and magic.

A bird with golden glowing feathers and eyes resembling jewels having great power because of the magic each of its feathers contain. Some folk tales say the firebird is a mystical bird seen flying around a king's garden at night stealing golden apples.

Modern fantasy has joined the firebird and Phoenix as one creature, but the firebird originally represented an everlasting magical torch, made of living fire, living light, while the Phoenix goes up in flames only in death to be reborn in the ashes.

The story of the firebird comes in many forms, but some say the firebird is a brightly coloured songbird while others say the firebird is just an ordinary bird flying around giving hope to those who need it.

Here, Michelle's words are the magical feathers as this collection of poetry takes flight to give hope to all in need and share notions of rebirth, beauty and magic. 'Firebird' in poetic prose is the songbird, the everlasting light and also as playfully a paradox as the legendary mythical creature stealing apples from the king.

FIREBIRD

WILD FOREST

Her heart is a kingdom
all on its own
ruled by a star
in the shape of her soul
a forest of wild
laced with silky elm
but cherished are those
to have entered this realm

"Every now and then allow yourself to give precedence to other dimensions of your being. Then fly darling, fly."

◆ • •••••••••••••••••••••• • ◆ • •••••••••••••••••••• • ◆

FIREBIRD

You'll find new constellations
when you look into her eyes
and far off distant lands
where the firebird flies
A firebird named Venus
with tail feathers like flames
composer of haunting music,
a thirst for hunger games
If you should get close enough
you'll see her eyes are jewels
All seeing crystal vision
and a firebird for a muse

✦ • ....• ✦ • ....• ✦

NAKED

Sometimes I drown in the emotions
I feel down to my bones
All my senses shaking
in rhythm to a heart that moans
Vibrations of a soul
intense yet barely breathing
Feeling naked to the world
And I wonder if I'm dreaming

PARALLEL DREAMING

Your hand touched my face
and past lives flashed before my eyes
Visions of you kissing my palms
in ancient Egyptian times
Suddenly it all makes sense
yet not quite any sense at all
this juxtaposition of contradiction
seems something paradoxical
we have swam through the deepest oceans
with tails similar to fish
in parallel universes our heartbeats echo
from some great abyss
We have sailed in seas of love
drifted different realms in many streams
and we have danced,
oh, how we dance
in all dimensions of my dreams

*"Allow yourself to feel intrigued
and aroused by beauty through
all of your senses."*

✦ • ···························• ✦ • ························• ✦

MAKING LOVE

I kissed the earth
with my bare feet
Reached high to touch the skies
found beauty all around
made love
with my eyes

✦ • •••••••••••••••••••••• • ✦ • •••••••••••••••••••• • ✦

SHINE

I will never let life's cruelties
harden up my heart
I'll breathe warmth into hope gone cold
and let light shine
through all my scars

SEPIA HORIZON

As the sun yawns into evening
shadows skip a sepia horizon
may you find something to believe in
sure, as daylight will shine again
As sunset drips into nighttime
and darkness pulls you close
whispering into your ear
like a long-lost playful ghost
I hope you are feeling grateful
reminded of treasures you keep
the kind you hold inside your heart
nurturing while you're asleep
And by the time it's morning
may the first thing you have heard
be pleasant thoughts accompanied
by sounds of a songbird
I pray memories that greet you
are nourishing your soul
and dance inside your mind
like a favourite story told
So while you fully waken
and the moon is seen yawning
may you celebrate your life
with beauty of day dawning

AWAKENING

Why does the moon pull me so
But you push me away
I wonder how I keep so still
When I can never stay
how is it my heart breaks
Whenever I start feeling whole
Why am I so very tired
while awakening my soul

✦ • ⋯⋯⋯⋯⋯⋯• ✦ • ⋯⋯⋯⋯⋯⋯• ✦

ALIGNMENT

At times I don't
remember to forget
Focus on the present moment
dream of what's to happen yet
Sometimes I forget to remember
the now in this story
Align with destiny instead
of my history

DEEPER

You do not need a mirror
to recognise you're worth it
All that you are
lies so much deeper
than any shiny surface

YOUNIVERSE

Can you feel
it breathe
inside of you
all that's good
and kind
and true
You are the world
the sky
moonlight
sunburst
Close your eyes
to see
you are
the universe

BENT NOT BROKEN

Find me at the edge
of the ocean
where my back breaks
against the tide
But leave me
in the depths
my spine will bend
when stars collide

✦•·················•✦•····················•✦

HATCHLING

Every night she went to bed
with pain from her soul aching
listening to sounds
of a gentle heart that's breaking
Until she understood
why her heart was filled with cracks
It had to open up to free the love
now ready to hatch

> *"Rules are made to be broken*
> *Not hearts."*

WINGS

In time
your wounds
will turn to wisdom
and from wise things
shall grow wings

✦ • ·················· • ✦ • ·················· • ✦

INTUITIVE SOULS

We are gentle
gods and goddesses
with winged spirits
born to ride
the wild winds of passion
to find adventure
When we love
it's completely, compassionately,
but never possessively
and we always listen
to the whispering wisdom
of our intuitive souls

✦ • ·························· • ✦ • ···················· • ✦

THIRD EYE

I was blessed
with three eyes
I look with two
The other is for seeing

SOUL CONNECTING

I like it when my soul
steps quietly outside of me
to breathe in all the magic
feel each pulse of energy
Making me slow down
time to catch my breath
absorbing every detail
so we gently reconnect

"I find myself at times overcome with
feelings I don't know how to feel."

MIND'S EYE

I sometimes feel things deeper
than my body and each bone
Somewhere my mind can see
a place my soul has known
Those who feel with every fibre
of their conscious being
find peace and love in all that's wild
Visions through instinctual seeing

EMPATH

Don't tell me you are an empath
unless you've felt the breeze brush your bones
or you can feel the vibrations of heartbeats
from whoever sits closest to you.
Have you tasted the salt of another's soul
as their tears drop upon your own cheeks?
Do not tell me you're an empath
until you have tried to tear your own heart
from your chest to stop the hurting.
And even then, don't tell me,
I'll know.

✦ • ....• ✦ • ....• ✦

BREATHE

And when your world stops
they all carry on
a reminder again
of how you don't belong

All of the things
you once held so dear
seem out of reach in times
of crippling fear

Your heart feels heavy
it's dragging you down
into an abyss
you wish you could drown

But you fight to hang on
in the darkest depth
as you swim in your thoughts
while your lungs search for breath

When every emotion
has hit, cried and seethed
you'll be yearning the most
to be able to breathe

HEAVENLY HEARTS

Every time a teardrop falls
for those we loved and lost
it's a little piece of liquid heaven
upon our cheek

For heaven is a place
there inside the heart
where all your precious memories
go to speak

✦ • .... • ✦ • .... • ✦

SENSITIVITY

I might talk over you
blissfully unaware
without knowing it's annoying
but don't think I don't care
I just get excited
to share all my thoughts
and this mouth runs ahead
of my minds obstacle course
And yes, I may fidget
bounce, twirl my hair
not know which way to turn
when I'm already there
But I feel everything
from my head to my toes
even Earth spinning
that's how
sensitivity goes

*"Find which life experiences bring
you inspiration and energy,
then romance your own soul."*

✦ • ⋯⋯⋯⋯⋯⋯•✦• ⋯⋯⋯⋯⋯⋯•✦

TRUE BEAUTY

When her past
proved that love lies
She fell in love
with the beauty
of her own truth

DEVOURED

I fed the wolf inside my heart
with the wildness from my soul
He devoured each and every part
and stayed to keep me whole

WARMTH OF WOLVES

She runs inside me, some wild thing
the warmth of wolf beneath my skin
chasing my energy like an echo

She burns inside me, I feel the sting
waiting for her howl to sing
alluring me to somewhere deep below

My lover comes to me, primal sensuality
stirring all my senses
as he meets her there, some wild thing

Seeking shooting stars within
exploding
The warmth of wolves beneath my skin

THE FRAY

You fray my emotional edges
slowly removing velvet
maybe not you at all
my own heart sets me up to fall

I'll let go of expectations
in all of my relations
they're far too heavy to hold
for this weary heart and soul

I want to love wild, carefree,
unconditionally
embracing love divine
the collective of humankind

Consciously
rebirth
nurtured
by Mother Earth

SAFE

I get lost sometimes
for a little while
but look for me
behind my smile
And if it seems
I'm worlds apart
please keep me safe
inside your heart

ONCE UPON A TIME

If you listen carefully
you can hear all the stories
especially the ones without words
In smiles lighting sparklers in eyes
and spreading a softness across faces
In forehead kisses where safety
holds you tightly wrapped in love
In hearts escaping through eyes
falling upon cheeks
and in that place where there's no time
to walk upon
only dancing under starlight

✦ • .... • ✦ • .... • ✦

SLOW DANCING

And love is the reason
my intensity finds stillness
in some moments
still learning how to slow dance
to the sounds of my soul

KISSING SCARS

I want to love you
with the fire
of a million burning stars
I want my lips
to press against you
kissing all your scars
I want to touch you
your body and your heart
But tell me will you love me
Every broken part

GLOW

You stay in darkness
just to let me shine
but when I touch you
I feel a part of myself being touched
And I know I have never
or won't ever
be able to glow as bright
as this again
without you

HEART LIGHT

Look for the light
inside my heart
I switched it on for you
To show you your way home

WORK OF ART

I like the lines upon your face
they tell a story of your laughter
and all the years etched in your bones
make for happy ever after
Each tiny freckle on your skin
tells of once upon a time
and when you're smiling from your cheeks
without reason or rhyme
Every little sound your voice echoes
like perfect poetry
the rhythm of your heartbeat
is sweet music to me
But most of all I seem to fall
for thoughts straight from your heart
And all the pieces of your soul
make you a work of art

FOREVER

I could

live forever

in just

one moment

with you

✦ • •••••••••••••••••••••••••• • ✦ • •••••••••••••••••••••• • ✦

SKIN TO SKIN

Free your body
from your clothes
Let them fall like petals
to the floor
you really won't be needing those
when I hold you
like you've not been held before
Hug me so close
feel skin to skin
no telling
where you or I begin
Let us be a circle
while shivers send
goosebumps to flesh
where there's no end
Circle shaped love
no finish or start
simply souls
heart to heart

THINKING OF YOU

If sensuality
leaves fingerprints
upon my skin today
you'll know
I've thought of you

UNTOUCHED

I love how you caress
every inch of me

without even
touching

All my senses
caressed

How your eyes have me
undressed

No one touches me
quite like

the way
you don't

✦ • •••••••••••••••••• • ✦ • • •••••••••••••••• • ✦

TOUCHED

Did you hear the quietness?
Can you see the dark?
Did you taste the water?
Can you feel my heart?
Did you kiss my soul,
While I was looking at the dark?
'Cause when I listened to the silence
I think you touched my heart

ALL THAT'S PRETTY

I like all that's pretty and shiny
and I might speak with a glittering tongue
I like cars, sex and rock 'n' roll
but when all that's said and done
I love with every inch of my being
if you can catch my gist
I look for the rawness in people
I'll love you unconditionally if you're on my list
Give me the part of you that leaves you terrified
the wildness in your heart that breathes
the bits of your soul that know only darkness
all of you that hurts and bleeds
And yes, we can have pretty and shiny
drive fast and have spine-tingling sex
but when we're alone under the moonlight
I'll be loving your darkness the best

✦ • ⋯⋯⋯⋯⋯⋯⋯• ✦ • ⋯⋯⋯⋯⋯⋯• ✦

CHAMPAGNE SOUL

I want to write song lyrics
sing from my soul
drink champagne
and never grow old

✦ • ⋯⋯⋯⋯⋯⋯⋯• ✦ • ⋯⋯⋯⋯⋯⋯⋯• ✦

YOUNG HEARTS

Oh, how we miss our youth
Young hearts full of trust
Days thinking about nights
filled with fun and lust
Nothing brought us down
no worrying or fuss
just wishing for the weekend
to come quicker than us

DRAGON

She has the Soul
of a dragon
with a heart
beating fire

BURNING BEAUTY

Whisper the wind
in a language of love
earth below my feet
skies up above
Sunshine's kiss
moonlight's caress
call of the wild
awaken each sense
Fire in my heart
stars in my eyes
burning beauty
deep inside

INTANGIBLE

Sometimes she feels
something is missing
not a piece of her heart
or any feeling of inadequacy
But her soul misses
something intangible
the way a star misses the darkness
come each morning

✦•·····················•✦•·····················•✦

FREQUENCY

Love is
a tangible intangibility
I heard whispered in the stars
A resonance of creation
synchronised vibrations
of hearts
Natural frequencies
creating special music
Love is poetry, energy
Its own kind of magic

SUN KISSED

I talk to statues
and dance with the stars
I always roll the windows down
when driving fast in cars
I sing to the moon
sigh at kisses from the sun
And sometimes late at night
I count headlights one by one

KINGS AND SHADOWS

He is his own breed of warrior, a song
with or without someone to sing
Noble Knight, a king alone
or beside a queen
When he starts feeling lost
and shadows begin to creep
he follows light inside his soul
to put darkness to sleep

FORGIVENESS

A primitive force runs
behind her eyes
burying in a graveyard
where every painful memory lies
bones of the past
they resurface now and then
but her heart is brave
beating strength
for those she has forgiven

BURIED BONES

I have buried so much of my past, it's true
but sometimes I catch a glimpse of my heart
digging its way to you

"The thing about love and pain
they sometimes feel the same."

✦ • ⋯⋯⋯⋯⋯• ✦ • ⋯⋯⋯⋯⋯• ✦

SUMMER LOVE

The warm breeze strokes her skin
sunshine kisses her soul
She lets summertime sadness begin
as her memories come out for a stroll

HOME COMING

All my life I was stared at
like a statue in an art gallery
Although I appreciate the arts
all I ever wanted
was for someone to look at me
like maybe I am home

"All eyes on her when she enters a room.
While she only ever has her eyes on you."

GRACE

She spent her lifetime hiding
behind an angel face
So, on her way to heaven
She learnt to walk through hell
with grace

"Be an angel
Always choose kindness
Live so passionately
You could raise hell."

BESIDE OURSELVES

Sometimes the devil
speaks with eloquence
in a gentle voice
And angels walk
next to us
without wings

STARS WIDE OPEN

The world has many layers
and when stars open like eyes
the universe breathes in whispers
singing softly 'kiss the skies'

"Please don't pick flowers for me
I don't want their wild to wilt then die
I'd like a bouquet of stars
plucked directly from the sky."

LOST STAR

No, she's no damsel in distress
waiting for a knight
She is but a lost star
looking for her night

WISH

And maybe
a star falls
to make a wish
upon you

MOTHER'S KISS

She touched me
and I smelled daisies
and long grass
felt baby's breath
caress my neck
She smiled
and I could taste
sweet dreams
looking like home
upon her lips

ANGEL BABIES

Not all mothers get the chance
to watch their children grow
their babies found forever
sleeping sound inside their soul
But angel babies stay in hearts
of mums and dads always
to remind them of their strength
through their darkest days
Though little flags won't get the chance
to ever become unfurled
tiny footprints will forever make
big marks upon the world

PIECES OF MY HEART

When a soul breaks
it won't break even
fragments might fly to hell
other parts to heaven
But if my heart should break
I hope it scatters freely
so wherever you may go
you'll find pieces of me

REBEL SOULS

She is made of spirits free
and rebel souls
Every place
a wild heart goes

*"She is a gentle power radiating quiet
light, a paradox of all that could be
wrong with right."*

✦ • ⋯⋯⋯⋯⋯⋯•✦• ⋯⋯⋯⋯⋯•✦

IN BETWEEN

Tip of an arrow
blade of a knife
turning scars into weapons
cutting my way through life
Piercing love through my heart
carving paths to my dreams
growing wings from the wounds
Loving me in between

GROW

I picked my heart up
from the floor
and cupped her in my hands

made a promise of no more
felt my heartbeat
kiss my palms

And to this day
a promise kept
my heart stays here inside my chest

making love in all the hearts I know
to teach the world
how love can grow

"I have pulled beauty from their eyes
to shoot it through blind hearts
losing sight sometimes
of myself along the way."

BLIND LOVE

I hope you get to know
the presence of the stars
and reach for them in dreams

Feel little hairs upon your arms stand up
when you've been touched
by moonbeams

Goosebumps will dance
to happy sounds
let the magic of music begin

Your heart beats warmth
as sunshine drops
kisses upon your skin

Embrace the world
with love and joy
a special quality

The best things in life
felt from the heart
where you'll find truest beauty

NURTURE

Some leave you for dead
and bury you in dirt
others hold you close
all through the shame and hurt
When you are held so tight
you'll become a brand new bud
Nurture each other as you grow
then bloom out of the mud

*"My heart tilts toward you
like a flower to face the sun."*

RECOVERY

They say we accept
the kind of love we think we deserve
But some just adapt to the only kind of love
they've been shown

So, when anxiety and self-doubt
lay down with our bodies
they become
the lovers we have known

When nightmares are all
that hold us through the night
We quickly learn to love
our monsters

Once exposed
to love with light
we'll learn how soon
the heart recovers

"We each carry around our hopes
and hurts
while daydreams dance upon our skin
And healing can hurt too
but lets all the light in."

BLISSFUL

Dip your toes into her mystic depth
be dizzy in her exhaled breath
feel warmed from the glow of her hearts fire
dance to the rhythm of her desire
Sing to her soul's melody
be ever surprised by her beauty
hold her when she's vulnerable
catch her every time she'll fall
Bless her each night before sleep
show her promises are to keep
leave her always with your kiss
love her through sad times
and the bliss

"Doing that thing you do
makes my soul stir deep
kiss me, touch me, love me
I'll be yours to keep."

◆ • ···················· • ◆ • ···················· • ◆

ENERGY OF EARTH

Peaceful and calming now
he vibes with energy of earth
but when a warrior is born
it is not an easy birth
He has been broken open
leaving storms in his wake
allowing himself to heal
and find beauty through the break

✦ • •••••••••••••••••••• ✦ • •••••••••••••••••• • ✦

WARRIOR WINGS

She opened her heart
which made it crack
and though no wings were folded
on her back
right there where her heart
split in two
you'll see how
warrior wings grew

*"I don't wear precious jewels
but it's been said I have a heart of gold
I won't stretch the truth
though carry stories still untold
I myself
am made from tiny pearls of poetry
moments feeling bliss, 11:11 wish
and source energy."*

BURIED TREASURE

I have been many versions of myself
had to dig deep to find the woman I am now
but there's no going back again
those I left at the surface will remain behind
Yesterday does not recognise me
and tomorrow I am yet to meet
So today I dive into my depths
and find more of me to treasure

WOLF CRY

She has Wild Moon Woman qualities
seeking only love and truth
giving her heart to genuine loyalties
tired of those who only cry Wolf

"She has a heart so wild
The moon howls to her."

◆ • ⋯⋯⋯⋯⋯⋯⋯ • ◆ • ⋯⋯⋯⋯⋯⋯⋯ • ◆

SOUL SPEAK

You didn't say a thing
had no song to sing
and still you're all I heard
speaking without a word

Your eyes, they tell me when
to love you more, but then
the language of your soul
is all I need to know

✦ • ⋯⋯⋯⋯⋯⋯• ✦ • ⋯⋯⋯⋯⋯⋯• ✦

US

I miss you.
I miss the conversations we don't have
I miss the way you'd say I'm beautiful
one word said over and over billions of times
throughout every language
but made more aesthetic dripping from your tongue.
Oh, I miss your tongue, how it caressed my own
and the echoes of words not spoken stirring on its tip
Sometimes I think you miss me too
although you'd not admit it, not really
I'll bet no one else could ever say
"I love you", quite like the way I didn't
But I will always carry a piece of you with me
Anyone who gets close enough to me
will on some occasion
get a glimpse of you
even though we never really knew an 'us'.
Even though 'we' were beautiful.

"I dusted off the fingerprints
you left inside my soul
But they'll stay inked
inside my heart
replacing parts you stole."

FRAGMENTS OF MY HEART

There's a place deep inside of you
filled with little pieces of me
A mouthful of my kiss's memory,
texture of my touch, my poetry

Fragments of my heart
left behind for all to see
And no-one can truly know you
without too knowing
parts of me

BEAUTIFUL SOULS

While most might only feel
the soft breeze from your flight
I can also see your wings

When you open your heart's vision
you'll start seeing souls
and other beautiful things

"Wrap someone in a hug
open your heart
when you open your arms."

✦ • ⋯⋯⋯⋯⋯⋯⋯• ✦ • ⋯⋯⋯⋯⋯⋯• ✦

BLUSHED

Paint me all the patterns of your thoughts
dream of me in colours of your heart
Etch my fingerprints into your bones
so you will feel my touch while we're apart
Sign my name across your soul
when it comes time for you to write me
Keep me always on your mind
blushed with shades of poetry

"I dream in colours
that have yet to be painted."

WILD SKY

You kissed me
under a wild sky
And I can't help
but wonder
Was it always wild
or did that kiss
make it so?

ONE

My lips will be the earth
yours will be the sky
And when the sun dips
below the horizon
May the earth and sky
meet as one

SPARKLES

Yes, I have smiled when I really wanted to cry
I've radiated happiness when I've been unhappy
I have given love when my own heart has been aching
I've forgiven those who perhaps do not deserve forgiveness
I have stayed calm in moments of despair
I've given comfort to others when I have needed comforting
I have been told that I have tact to tell someone to go to hell
and make them feel excited for the journey
That I have an iron fist in a velvet glove
Yes, I sugar coat
But I am me
I'm never fake
I tell the truth always
I am strong
I believe in kindness
I believe in fucking sparkles
And I will sprinkle them like love
everywhere I can.

AUTHENTIC

I found a door to my heart
I'd never opened before
it led me to some places
where I could see my worth
I met Self reflection
and her friend Creativity
they showed me pictures of my character
where I met Integrity
She introduced me to her sister kindness
and taught me to be true
now I'm meeting Authenticity
so, I can grow and then teach you

THORNS IN OUR SIDES

I see you and your suffering
sometimes you're too tired to speak
I see strength of a warrior soul fighting
when your body is feeling weak
I see tears dropping silently
behind each 'I am fine'
I feel your aches, your skin on fire
because your pain is just like mine

*"Some will only see you
through rose coloured glass
but me, I feel the beauty
of your thorns."*

OUR STORY

I saw you with my heart
from the very start
the smile in your soul
the heart in your gold
I knew there and then
our story has no end

*"How can I see such a rugged man
to be so soft and shimmery?" I asked*

*"Because you saw his soul." said my
heart*

*"Why would such a man show me his
soul?"*

"Because he has seen yours."

WHITE FIRE

There's a white fire
in the sky
to light the way for you and I
Through any darkness, sorrow, gloom
fill hearts of glass
and drink the moon

"I want to drink moonlight
bathe in flower petals
wear the earth, sleep in streams
and taste the stars."

✦ • ....• ✦ • ....• ✦

LITTLE SIPS

I like the sound of thoughts
and the taste of certain words
I love the feeling in my heart
as though it's filled with tiny birds
I particularly like the way
some stories seem to look
and the music I hear playing
from deep inside a book
But what I like the most
is the soul inside your kiss
it has me intoxicated
like tasting stars in little sips

MOON FLOWER

She is a rare soul
knew it as a child
always awake dreaming
often seen running wild
She listened to colours
and knew things too soon
a rare heart, like a flower
that's grown on the moon

✦ • ....• ✦ • ....• ✦

SURVIVAL

When I go to my own depths
I wonder who might look for me
Whose soul will I sleep inside
Who'll keep me in their poetry?
If you hold me in your heart,
I'll return to you
and turn drowning into floating
'Cause surviving Is what I do

"I've survived some pain
that sometimes put my heart on hold
my soul has always carried
secrets never told
This year we have decided
to let our spirit fly
Let go of all that's heavy
(my heart, my soul and I)."

◆ • ••••••••••••••••••• • ◆ • ••••••••••••••••••• • ◆

SUN FIRE

Deep inside me grows a love
stronger than a thousand suns
When it touches my skin
I'll be a Soul on Fire

MOON SOUL

If my heart
is the sun
my soul the moon
It will never matter
you left so soon
Even when you can't be
I know you're the one
sure as my soul's the moon
And my heart the sun

"If the moon is the soul of the sky
You must be my moon."

LOVE IS THE WARRIOR

Love is a warrior
standing proud and tall
ready for battles
with hammer, shield and sword
Hammer to seal
promises tight
shield to protect
from day throughout night
Sword to be drawn
only in
dire need
because love is the warrior
Not a knight
on a steed

QUIESCENT

You kissed my neck
cracked open my soul
and breathed poetry to life
in places lain dormant for centuries

"I have loved you longer than this life."

✦ • •••••••••••••••••••••••••• • ✦ • •••••••••••••••••••••••••• • ✦

THINGS THAT MADE ME SMI :)E TODAY

a daughter's kiss
a stream of sunshine
through the springtime showers
Feet up over the railway lines wish
good books
and fresh wildflowers

"Be kind
Live simply
Expect little
And don't forget
to smile."

✦ • .... • ✦ • .... • ✦

HONEY AND THE BEE

The grace in my stride
the swing in my hips
my sense of pride
colour of my lips
the thoughts in my mind
my tender touch
compassionate and kind
caring so much
My heart is gentle
my soul so strong
mellifluous voice
just like a song
the taste of my kiss
the scent of my hair
much more than this
but baby beware
my tongue can be sweet
or sting like a honeybee
the truth in my words
the woman in me

✦•••••••••••••••••••••••••••✦•✦•••••••••••••••••••••••••✦

COUNTRY ROADS

Her skin is a silken city
lit up with electricity
made of party lights, long nights,
dancing shoes and words so pretty

Her heart is a castle standing strong
filled with hope and a haunting love song
tall towers, scattered flowers
and stories
from days now long gone

Her mind is a world of its own
twisting roots to gardens overgrown
realms of romance, a sensual slow dance
Warrior queen
upon her throne

Her soul is both young and old
gypsy feet, secrets not told
peace personified, mix of gentle yet wild
The music played travelling
a country road

"I found my gypsy wings
And danced into the sky."

VAGABOND

I found a home
amongst the stars
laid me down
my vagabond heart
And the moon ...
                she loved me to sleep

"I want to live in the night
Play with the moon
dance among the stars
run wild with the wolves."

✦•·····················•✦•·····················•✦

DON'T

You don't have to say
you love me
you do not even
have to care
Just hold me
with your eyes
and I will
love you there

*"You didn't have to break my heart
to find yourself
I would have torn it open for you."*

✦ • .... • ✦ • .... • ✦

HOLDING HOPE

I stared hope
in the face
questioning her truth
But she held me tight and said
"I'm always here for you."

"Hope is the dreaming
your soul stitches into
all the cracks of your heart."

◆ • ⋯⋯⋯⋯⋯⋯⋯⋯⋯ • ◆ • ⋯⋯⋯⋯⋯⋯⋯ • ◆

STAR SEEDS

Every time her heart would break
she'd send broken pieces to the sky
fill herself with love instead
the kind nobody could deny
So each time now you wonder
about your very own heart scars
look to the night and dream about
a girl who planted stars

DREAMER'S HEART

For the love of dreams
commit to them
For dreams of love
submit to them
When dreamer's hearts
love all they do
rest assured
dreams will come true

SOUL PATH

Wherever I may be
Wherever else I go
There's just one path I need
The wisdom of my soul

WORDLY WISE

I don't have
a thirst for knowledge
but a hunger for life
And wisdom is born
through the labour
of experience

✦ • ⋯⋯⋯⋯⋯⋯⋯ • ✦ • ⋯⋯⋯⋯⋯⋯ • ✦

ANCIENT BEAUTY

I've felt your touch before somewhere
where ancient beauty breathes
The universe, she met us there
with petals, stems and leaves
But lifetimes seemed to pass us by
and little did we know
We had to first learn all the lessons
for our souls to bloom and grow

*"Tribal goddess
Where are you from?"*

*"The earth, the sea
and my ancestors' bones."*

GENTLE

Her altruistic nature
makes for part of her most
intimate essence

with a core value
of kindness
and always good intents

When she looks at you
her eyes are filled
with loving care

because it's in her eyes
you'll see how gently
she carries her heart there

*"Soften my wild edges
but leave my spirit free."*

✦ •✦ •✦

HER

There was music sweet
There was every heartbeat
There were wounds and scars
There was the moon and stars
There was poetry
and profound beauty
There was each sunrise
There were stories hidden behind eyes
There were pretty sights
Party invites, city lights
There was an angels whisper
and then ...

There was her.

HIM

He was just like
that last page
of a book
that makes your soul sigh
and all you can do
is stare ...

Wishing for more.

COCOON

Sometimes feelings
take a hold of me
with winding roots
like I'm a tree
Yet my heart
remains the butterfly
wings made of dreams
destined to fly
I once was caged
now I am free
Cocooned
not caged
Only now
I see

BUTTERFLY KISS

Velvety lashes
crown her eyes
resembling wings
of butterflies
A glimpse your way
one little wink
you'll catch your breath
no time to think
She'll captivate you
like the queen she is
with a graceful wave
of the butterfly kiss

CHARM

Eyelash lace
velvet breath
starlight kiss
angel's footstep
Siren song
silver in a wishing well
The woman is a walking,
talking spell

BELLADONNA

Beautiful Donna
Lady of the dark
Fluttering through the night
like a soaring skylark
What you'd give for a taste
of witchcraft in a kiss
pretty but poison
those venomous lips

✦•••••••••••••••••••••••••••••••••••✦•••••••••••••••••••••••••••••••✦

WARRIOR WOLF

She is a warrior
who let the wolves swallow her whole
she had to be consumed
for a taste of her own soul
So now she breathes inside a chest
pulling arrows from a heart
in such a way you'd never tell
her or the wolf apart

✦ • ⋯⋯⋯⋯⋯⋯• ✦ • ⋯⋯⋯⋯⋯⋯• ✦

LOVE STORY

She is just a girl
with stars in her eyes
Storms in her heart
wolves beneath her skin
and a love story soul

TWO FLAMES

I sometimes wonder why
I taste your tears if you should cry
The salt of your very soul
flavoured just like my own
Now and then you think of me
I feel it by your energy
No matter near or far
we'll speak a language heart to heart
Each of us alone do not begin
but together we have no ending
And if our hearts run out of breath
Two flames will together rest

SOUL LANGUAGE

I see hearts
in the contour of lips
the rosiness
of a cheek

I feel energy
in all that's breathing
and I listen
when souls speak

✦ • ⋯⋯⋯⋯⋯⋯⋯⋯• ✦ • ⋯⋯⋯⋯⋯⋯⋯• ✦

SENSORY

(A Sense Story)

Sometimes I hear my heartbeat
throbbing in my head
so loud I'm kept awake
guess I'll sleep when I am dead
Some say I'm too sensitive
they think I must be weak
if battles fought were glimpsed by them
they'd turn the other cheek
My senses are awakened
and often go to war
fighting with my feelings
neither keeping score
But though I feel each hurt
viciously intense
oh how I'm blessed with my capacity
to love with every sense

SLIDER PHENOMENON

Everything has energy
I feel it hard and it feels me
clocks stop, light bulbs blow
wherever I may seem to go
But music keeps my sanity
It's magic kind of sets me free
soothes my soul
and comforts me
Fills my heart with poetry

BUKOWSKI KNEW

She is so much more than pretty
or any other label
She is resilient
and forever more than able
She is magical madness
and soulful desire
She's aware of her own truth
(Charles knew)
there's no lie in her fire

✦ • ⋯⋯⋯⋯⋯⋯•✦• ⋯⋯⋯⋯⋯•✦

BLEEDING IN INK

Words burn beneath my skin
my mouth plays with tastes of ashes
poetry breathes flames in my soul
fluttering from my lashes
Bruises linger on my legs
shaped like your fingertips
little purple poems of lust
memories lick at my lips
Wolves howling in my heart
keep my spirit balanced
and when I'm bleeding dreams
in ink to paper
they smile and call it talent

FIRESTARTER

I'm not broken anymore
put pieces back together
walked through a new door
Left behind fragments
that no longer fit
burned bridges on my way
danced in fires I had lit
No, I'm not broken anymore
too full of life
to be broken hearted
I'm shining bright
from the flames raging
in fires my soul started

✦ • •••••••••••••••••••••••• • ✦ • •••••••••••••••••••••••• • ✦

FIREBIRD

ABOUT THE AUTHOR

Michelle Schaper, from Western Australia, works as a support worker/caregiver for disabilities, (or as she says, 'enhancing people's abilities.') She is a mentor/advocate for mental health and domestic violence and has written poetry since her childhood.

You'll find more of Michelle's work at:
facebook.com/chellessoulpoems on Facebook
@michellesoulkissing on Instagram.

www.ingramcontent.com/pod-product-compliance
Lightning Source LLC
Chambersburg PA
CBHW071009120626
46546CB00003B/1007